The Unfathomable Theology of Fishing

*Other books by Raymond H. Haan,
published by Wipf and Stock*

SINGING THE GAMUT
A Motley Clutch of Poems and Verse

WORD SONGS AND WHIMSIES
A Nest of Poems and Verse

ALPHABETICAL FROLIC
Verse Pictures of Our Twenty-Six Scamps and Saints
Illustrated by Chris Cook

The Unfathomable Theology of Fishing

a diverse collection of poems

RAYMOND H. HAAN

RESOURCE *Publications* • Eugene, Oregon

THE UNFATHOMABLE THEOLOGY OF FISHING
A Diverse Collection of Poems

Copyright © 2021 Raymond H. Haan. All rights reserved. Except for brief quotations in critical publications or reviews, no part of this book may be reproduced in any manner without prior written permission from the publisher. Write: Permissions, Wipf and Stock Publishers, 199 W. 8th Ave., Suite 3, Eugene, OR 97401.

Resource Publications
An Imprint of Wipf and Stock Publishers
199 W. 8th Ave., Suite 3
Eugene, OR 97401

www.wipfandstock.com

PAPERBACK ISBN: 978-1-6667-0337-5
HARDCOVER ISBN: 978-1-6667-0338-2
EBOOK ISBN: 978-1-6667-0339-9

07/06/21

I dedicate this little book to the joyful memory of four friends,
Clifford Kohlbeck, Richard Herrema,
Jerome Smith, and Ronald Kooistra—
each an unfading gift.

Contents

Acknowledgment	ix
Introduction	xi
The Unfathomable Theology of Fishing	1
Island	3
Flights	4
Departure	5
Grit	7
Running	8
Invitation	9
Shirts	10
Hope	12
Abuse	13
God's Secret	14
Nostalgia	15
Longing	16
Puzzle	17
Delight	18
Charlie Chipmunk and the Condo Queen	20
Tether	22
Molting	23
Cataract	24
Friends	25
Stuck	27
Eloquence	28

Paradox	29
No Emmaus	30
Demon	31
Theology on the Freeway	32
Bumps	35
Clean	36
Dinner Upside Down	37
Monochrome Dirge	39
Bereaved	40
The Gardener	41
Today's Tea	42
The Seed	43
Treasure	44
Two Tableaus	45
Bloodhound	47
Supple and Snug	48
Corpus Christi	49
Illustration	50
Detour	51
Wood Work	53
Dejection	54
Purpose	55
Perversion	56
Place of Peace	57
Crooked Cross Stitch	58
Survival	60
Golden Dawn	61
Oxygen	62

Acknowledgment

Once again I inscribe my gratitude to Kathleen Herrema, whose precise and patient angling in these verbal waters fished out flaws small and great. Defects yet lurking in the depths of this volume exist because the author failed to yield to her fishing expertise. (It should be noted that she has never adopted the practice of catch and release.)

Introduction

The year 2020 will hardly be remembered as a time of optimism or festivity, and the reasons for that are too well known and too distressing to catalogue here. If this scattering of poems in any measure reflects the soberness, uncertainty, and pervasive unhappiness of 2020, that has not been the intention. The plan of this and previous collections of poems has been to let each poem reveal the author's idea or emotion on the day of writing—without adhering to a single theme. So, if this collection seems somewhat dark or if the intermittent lighter poems seem out of place, the author asks your indulgence.

The Unfathomable Theology of Fishing*

II

Because the Lord knew where the fish were,
one morning His disciples tugged to the shore in Galilee
a netful of one hundred fifty-three:
a whole kingdom of large fish.
Of course, He knew exactly where to find the human fish, as well—
the nibblers, the bottom feeders,
the hungry, the skittish, or the tender-mouthed.
So, He fished a nibbler from a sycamore tree,
he found bottom feeders at suppers,
and his sharp but gentle hook secured
the empty, water-carrying woman at the well.
His line of love drew in Legion, the demoniac—
who, like the water-carrying woman,
became both fish and fisher.

Varied are God's fishing methods, and mysterious—
as with Samson or Nebuchadnezzar or Jonah.
As for Jonah, he set out on God's expedition to Nineveh—
but only after God's great fish caught him,
sunk into the black and weedy deeps of the Mediterranean,
only after he spent three days of horror and mortification
in the stinking stomach of that fishing fish

---

* The first poem bearing this title is published in *Word Songs and Whimsies,* Wipf and Stock, 2020.

(maybe with repulsive roommates),
only after it spit Jonah onto the seashore—
who knows? maybe in disgust or relief.
Then, off to Nineveh plodded Jonah,
and for forty days he trawled, drawing God's strong net
over that depraved and drowning mass of human fish.
And after those days God gathered Nineveh from its sea of sin.

Yet outside the city's thick brick walls
flapped and floundered God's slippery fisherman,
rebellious in his useless booth of branches,
angry and faint beside God's worm-smitten, withered gourd,
hoping for no harvest of souls,
but wishing instead for all heaven to break loose
on the city he hated and had helped to save,
hoping to see some fierce fire, some boiling brimstone
consume the place, as it did Sodom and Gomorrah.
How God netted His skittish and sassy fisherman no one knows.
God keeps His secrets.

> To this day God knows where His fish swim—
> knows their shallowness or awful depths—
> and as He casts out line and hook,
> He calls His fish, each one by name.
> In fact, their names are written
> on the hand that firmly holds
> His deep, inescapable,
> unbreakable,
> gentle
> net.

Island

In all this round and whirling sphere
where lies a land of shining peace?

In all this dizzy, spinning world
the fires of conflict still increase.

Is there some gentle, tranquil place
far off from frenzy's flame and dart?

Go seek an island, safe, serene—
and let that refuge be God's heart.

Flights

Two Haiku

I

A silent sparrow's
flitting shadow disappears
across grey, tired snow.

II

Alabaster dove,
winging now in sapphire sky,
your sweetness lingers.

In memory of my friend Cliff Kohlbeck

Departure

"Goodbye, my friend. I'll be back next week."
"Goodbye."
Down the long, narrow hallway I walk,
knowing that his eyes are on me as I go,
knowing, as I wave and turn the corner,
that he will be standing before his door, waving in return.
And so it is.

Today he looks far away and small
as he stands in his burgundy shirt before his door,
waving and sending a faint, "Goodbye!"
His smallness and distance seem vaguely prophetic.
Something surreal engulfs the moment,
maybe because he has just told me about yesterday,
about his fantasy or vision,
his walking through a place of enormous, white, inviting pillows.
He told me of the euphoria that had enveloped him,
the joy of feeling that his life was slipping
gently into the quiet whiteness of the next.
But then he told me that the euphoria had melted
into the pain of yesterday's sudden hospital visit—
pain of trying to get his mind straight about his anger then,
pain and remorse for hard words to medics and family members.
So, today pain is his ruler,
euphoria a white memory,
and sweet death a thwarted desire.

Looking down that long and narrow hall,
I see him waving, and I hear his weak, "Goodbye!"
He stands there before his door,
far away and small, distressed, confused,
wanting heaven, hating earth, and searching uncertainly for God.
Suddenly both vision and thought grow blurred,
so, quickly I turn and tug my limping heart
down the next long hallway,
seeing only what burns inside me:
the distant, diminished form of my friend,
standing lonesome in his burgundy shirt,
craving God's rescue and hardly able to ask for it.

Grit

A needed sink plug once I pried
from a discarded sink I spied
while strolling through the neighborhood.
I made it clean as best I could
when I came home, for it was soiled.
And so, I washed and sprayed and boiled
the dirty, uninviting thing,
then slipped it through the sink's bright ring.

But, though the plug seemed pure and clean,
never did it match the sheen
of chrome that sparkled in the sink.
Still, there it stayed—three years, I think.
And after those quick years slipped by,
I thought it might be good to try
again to make it bright and fit—
this time with baking soda's grit.
And, yes! a lovely shine appeared
just as the cloudy soda cleared.

The application for the day
was hardly very far away:
for stubborn, tarnished plugs like me
sometimes Grace needs grit for purity.

Running

The realm of medicine this day
brought me a word that wants to play.
Yes, *rhinorrhea* is the word,
a heavy term and rarely heard.

Now, wait. Do not in haste suppose
the word was fashioned to disclose
the pain of Rhino, horned beast
that in savannas loves to feast
on all those tough and tender grasses
that bones and muscles bring—and gasses.
There's no connection with the plumbing
that keeps a healthy rhino humming.

Though *rhinorrhea* as a word
strikes one as lofty and absurd,
it fills a need (we must suppose)
to substitute for *runny nose*.

For that's its meaning, after all.
So, sometime when at work or mall
or meeting you find droplets dripping,
and leave with nose up-tipped and sniffing,
your words, at least, will sound elite,
with scientific cant replete:
"It's not so bad; it always mends—
just chronic rhinorrhea, friends."

In memory of my friend Richard Herrema

Invitation

This morning modest Spring with gentle scent
slipped sweetly through the window of my room;
as pensive as the mourning dove it moved,
and wooingly it whispered as it went:

Your quiet friend has left us quietly,
for his sake come and freely welcome me
with heart-songs—warm and rich as his would be.

In memory of my friend Richard Herrema

Shirts

Unless you buy them at Good Will
and the wearer is unknown,
you do not put on another man's clothes
without some thought.

Five years ago my grandson Nick
took off his thin, threadbare shirt and gave it to me.
I still put on the tattered thing,
mostly to think of him and his impetuous affection.

But now I have received half a dozen shirts
after the death of my friend.
Far from being tattered,
they are clean, pressed, and handsome—
shirts I can put on with pride.

But I have not yet put them on,
mostly because he will be buried tomorrow,
and I cannot bring myself to do it.
Beyond that, clothes are intimate things:
Rich wore these shirts next to himself—they surrounded his body;
so before I wear them, I must accommodate to that idea.
Even then, when at last I gingerly button a shirt,
when I feel it enclose me,
I will have the odd sensation of putting on my friend's character—
his virtues, his idiosyncrasies, his habits of mind.

Now, David, wallowing in Saul's awkward armor,
knew the gift was useless, discarded it,
and took as his shield the fabric of faith.
St. Paul, knowing the greatest gift of clothing—
knowing, as David did, that not the clothing
but the Clothier gives beauty and protection,
made this stark metaphor:
"Put on Christ."

So, buttoning a shirt from Rich,
I will try to remember, just as he did,
to dress with ultimate propriety.

"Put on the Lord Jesus Christ . . . . " Romans 13:14

Hope

Robin joy
bursts orange
at break of morn,
like dreams.

Robins think
the world
has just been born,
it seems.

Abuse

Lone roadside willow, blowing there,
disorder, sadness you must bear:
assaulting wind transforms apace
your yellow branches' slender grace
to waif's untidy, tangled hair.
But who will see—and who will care?

God's Secret

Time is a master, not a friend;
invisible though time may be,
its iron rule declines to bend.

Time prisons us from birth to bier.
It covets nothing that we love,
yet snatches quick what we hold dear.

Time's being thwarts the lofty sage.
Its birth and death he cannot trace—
but maps time's passing, age by age.

When we in heaven's grandeur stand
and tiny time's cold clasp recall,
we'll smile—and maybe understand.

Nostalgia

Joy is like sand
   held in your hand:

grip as you may,
   it slips away.

Some few grains cling;
   like wasps they sting.

Longing

Soft gentleness of pastel pink and tan,
a dove takes rest within my dry rain trough.
Her rosy breast and greyish back expand
to shape her brief and broken-hearted song.
Her pink neck jerks; she cocks her shining head;
her black, uneasy eye makes careful search.
Then, lifting, quick she springs with ruby feet,
spreads out her white-etched wings, and skyward flies—
to seek, perhaps, like Noah's pilgrim dove,
a rest far off, where no dove ever mourns.

"Oh that I had wings like a dove! for then would I fly away, and be at rest. Lo, then would I wander far off, and remain in the wilderness. I would hasten my escape from the windy storm and tempest." Psalm 55:6—8

Puzzle

A fragile puzzle
is the heart:

although its scene
may be serene,

one piece removed,
it tears apart.

Delight

This sturdy, steaming English pot, an old and cherished gift,
filled with memories of evening tea festivities with Joe,
the giver of the pot, the giver of our tea-filled times together,
times when we listened to Dvorak, Elgar, or Saint-Saens,
as I drank the introductory tumbler of Manischewitz,
and as we then imbibed our tea, cup after cup, pot after pot—
with cookies, chocolate and abundant, which he pressed on me;

this fragrant, liquid amber in my cup,
from flush of bushes sun-bathed
on the hills of green Sri Lanka—
birthday tea it is from Phil and Jackie,
or maybe from Mandy and Chris or Julie;

this graceful cup, a Christmas thought from Kathy,
she herself a calm accompaniment
at tea through happy decades past:

all these provide companionship,
silent yet sweetly eloquent,
as I sit to think and work.

How simple the picture:
table, teapot, tea and cup.
Simple, yes, until one mines
the mysteries of space and time and love—
a union strong that fashions sweet delight
from things I see and touch and pour—
and things unseen I value more.

Charlie Chipmunk and the Condo Queen

An amoral fable based on facts amply amplified

Young Charlie Chipmunk, quick and lean,
desired to have his runway clean.
The Condo Queen's impatiens pots,
embellished with forget-me-nots
and sometimes a geranium,
annoyed his heart—and cranium.
Those pots deranged his daily path;
their placement sparked his chipmunk wrath.

As Charlie woke one summer day,
hope filled his soul. He planned to pay
a business call—to dig and glean
the plants owned by the Condo Queen.
And so it was. His hope-filled soul
by evening had achieved its goal:
he dug and chewed in vengeance hot,
and so brought death to every pot.

Observing from his nearby hole,
he smirked to have attained his goal.
The Condo Queen stood bathed in grief
for havoc wrought on root and leaf.
But suddenly her back went straight,
her gentle face showed hints of hate.
She disappeared; he could not see,
so Charlie scuttled up her tree.

The Queen returned in dreadful ire,
pronouncing maledictions dire,
but Charlie chuckled and felt smug,
delighting in the holes he'd dug.
What did she carry in her hand?
That gallon—was it safe and bland,
or was it toxic, rife with death,
robbing life by stealing breath?

Her lips compressed, her eyebrow arched,
directly to his hole she marched
with jug of soap and garden hose—
at which the heart of Charlie froze.
Now, trembling to achieve her goal,
she drained the jug into his hole
and then applied the hose with force
to purge malfeasance at its source.

As bubbles billowed from the ground
and covered all the lawn around,
smart Charlie Chipmunk in the tree
began to weep distressfully.
Alas! too late he came to see
the payment for perversity.
Yes, hope had filled his willful soul;
but soap now filled his private hole.

Coda:
Perhaps some aged sage, some clown, or literary fake
has said, "Ah, yes, my friends! Good morals do good fables make."
Yet let this most affecting tale bring one apt thought to mind:
in fables, as in life, good morals one can rarely find.

Tether

The pleasures of Satan's false freedom
                                                 reach
just to the end of his thick, pitch-black
                                                 leash.
Insipid they are, like watered-down.
                                                 wines,
and satisfy thinly, like imperfect
                                                 rhymes.

The tether of Grace, a feather to
                                                 feel,
draws stronger than cords of tough, twisted
                                                 steel,
draws long from pale earth to tables that
                                                 shine,
draws strong to God's joy—the feast of new
                                                 wine.

> *"I drew them with cords of a man, with the bands of love."*
> *Hosea 11:4*

> *"But I say unto you, I will not drink henceforth of this fruit of the vine until that day when I drink it new with you in my Father's kingdom." Matthew 26:29*

Molting

Gone the beguiling face of spring,
gone her dew-drenched blooms
and ravishing perfumes,
gone the freshness of her luscious youth.

Aging, wrinkling, subtle-scented summer
now warms old people on their
white-posted porches
and pink-edged patios—
old people, nodding in their chairs,
scarcely noting the few and muted songs
of robins molting in thickets and low branches,
molting as they wait to fly, new-feathered,
from fall's frost, from dark and songless winter.

Waiting, nodding in their chairs,
old people watch the passing cars
and hope for neighbors to come and talk—
old people, molting on their porches and patios,
contriving to ignore the coming frost
or musing on the valley to be crossed.

Cataract

Like a cataract they fall, tumbling,
churning, hurtling
over hard places,
plummeting
without restraint
(captive to
creation's
potent
gravity)
never pausing,
ever changing:
the wild, white
torrent of
swiftly-
plunging,
beautiful,
empty-full
years.

Friends

Paper clips
grow friendly
in their box.
    (They unite
    out of sight
    overnight.)

Hangers lock
and tangle
on the rod.
    (They grow bold,
    so they hold
    while you scold.)

Lids and jars
bond tight through
days or years.
    (All you do
    to unscrew
    can fail you.)

Jar and lid,
hangers, clips
mirror friends.
(Days grow old,
years unfold—
still they hold.)

"... *there is a friend that sticketh closer than a brother."*
Proverbs 18:24b

Stuck

A free alternative to Hallmark for your valentine

Let's simply say
you are the jar,
and I the lid.
The grooves of lid
and grooves of jar
must fit just right
for jar and lid
to bond quite tight.
And, yes, they do.
That's plainly why
I'mstucktoyou.

In memory of my friend Jerome Smith

Eloquence

Decades ago when trouble came,
my friend Jerome handed me some words—
seven unpretentious words
on a piece of folded tablet paper,
seven grade-school words of bare simplicity.

Jerome has gone, but not his words.
Of thought-filled things that people wrote
only his small sentence clings to memory.
Half a lifetime it has sounded in my mind:

> *You are my friend,*
> *no matter what.*

That was no fabrication of poetry,
no striving to be fluent or expressive,
no struggle to be memorable.
Eloquence of the heart it was—
and simple, bracing honesty.

Paradox

We part—we hug and kiss and cry;
we say, "So long," "Adieu," or "Ciao;"
we part—and sometimes wonder how,
but Jesus never said goodbye.

When Jesus rose from earth to sky
in splendor of His strength arrayed,
His gaping friends no grief displayed,
though Jesus had not said goodbye.

Unkindness was not Jesus' way:
He had no cause to say goodbye,
His friends no need to weep or sigh—
for though He left, yet did He stay.

"... I am with you always, even unto the end of the world."
Matthew 28: 20b

No Emmaus

When this pale dream dissolves,
and when the great last dawn has dawned,
then, my daughters, we will walk again—
in this same place, perhaps,
on smooth and velvet-mossy paths,
moving lightly over new and ever-vernal earth.

So let us count our countless walks as preludes—
shadows of that bright reality
in which our rambles might well be
as countless as eternity,
when, in each ever-opening flower,
in all the boundless, star-hung sky,
in every silver river, every tree,
the very face of God will shine perpetually.

Peace will be ours: no burning hearts, no fear of night,
no questionings, and no Emmaus in our sight;
for as the mossy paths of Paradise we tread,
Immanuel will break for us eternal bread.

Luke 24:13–31

Demon

A red blouse sways oddly,
black hair zigzags wildly,
white arms thrash like broken windmills,
white legs dance, then stagger.

Voice rasping through black teeth,
the girl leaps and lurches down the street,
first on one side, then on the other,
toward my parked car
like a mad or drunken dervish.

Surely she is possessed;
surely she is captive to a demon,
like the wretches pictured in scripture.

Yes, surely—
and the demon has a name:

    meth-

            am-

                   phet-

                         a-

                                mine.

Theology on the Freeway

Chicago, 1981

"What is *this*!"
Through the thickening twilight on Stoney Island Avenue
a blockade looms before the ramp to the Chicago Skyway.
Yet the ramp itself is clear and passable.
"What *is* this?" My eyes and heart rebel.

Our shortcut from the Dan Ryan Freeway has come to failure.
We have traveled from Minnesota; home is three hours away;
I am tired, as are my two young daughters.
We stop before the blockade, distressed and frustrated.
What must we do?
I decide to circumvent the impediment,
so I nurse the car over the littered ground beside the blockade,
then gingerly edge it up, up, up the high curb of the ramp.

A jolt. A sudden stop. What has happened?
I get out to look. The car rests on the high curb,
its power wheels hanging powerless in the air.
Now we are helpless, indeed;
lifting the car down would require five times my strength.

We sit in the car, feeling foolish and vulnerable
as darkness envelops the nearby shops and passing traffic.
The neighborhood is not welcoming and likely dangerous.
Should I risk leaving the girls while I seek help?
What help? A wrecker? Some body-builders?

What does the call to worship say?
Our help comes from the Lord,
who made heaven and earth.
Well, then, pray.

In the mirror I see a shiny black car, a Cadillac, drawing up.
The gigantic driver emerges and approaches my closed window.
"What are you doing?"
I open the window a bit and nervously explain.
"Put it in neutral."
The giant walks to the front of the car,
puts both hands underneath,
and with one enormous heave lifts the car
and lowers it off the curb.
Then he returns to the window and says,
"Follow me."

We do, away from the ramp, down a dark side street,
then down another—and more streets after that.
On and on we ride through ragtag neighborhoods,
wonderfully quiet under dim and intermittent street lights.
Dread and uncertainty creep over me:
what awful thing is this man planning?
If we stop following or if we lose sight of him,
we will be utterly, desperately lost.
Struggling between fear and hopelessness,
I intently follow the tall tail lights through the night.
Now the brake lights flare, and we slow.
The big man's arm points out the window to the left.
We turn and look. Yes! a ramp,

leading to the bright skyway above.
Looking ahead once more, we see the tail lights
of the black Cadillac evaporating into the night.

As the miles of freeway rush by,
I feel no tug toward fantasy,
but, rather, to theology,
the deep theology of Providence—
and my thoughts are hardly academic.

Bumps

Astride the bike or in the car
we crave a bumpless ride,
but manhole covers throng the streets—
they lurk on either side.

Those irksome brownish iron plugs
lie buried in our lanes;
they give us random thumps and bumps
and even psychic pains.

The engineers who plot the holes
have never had in mind
an ordered scheme or pattern plain:
their holes are not aligned.

Plugs scatter unpredictably;
but unlike leaves from trees
or pink clouds napping in deep sky,
they lack the power to please.

So, as you swerve—yet hit a plug,
you take an easy view:
"That's life—that's just the way it goes,"
then add, "Just so. . . . How true."

Clean

You wash your car;
dust multiplies.
You wash again;
birds desecrate.
Once more you wash,
but pines drip sap,
and fat bugs splash.
You wash again.

And so it is
with car or truck
or sink or floor,
or skin or clothes:
you wash and clean,
and wash once more—
you scrub and wash
your whole life long.

God's washing is not so.
He cleansed just once,
and though your spots return
and filth recurs,
one purging has sufficed
for every spot,
each filthy blot,
and every horrid stain.

Dinner Upside Down

Like the shoulders of Atlas
the crossbeams of the telephone pole
bear perpetual weight.
The grey old pole is cracked and bare,
except for rusted climbing spikes,
spaced, it seems, for Atlas himself.
They protrude from either side,
like slender, intermittent ears
or like the antennae of some gigantic insect.

A small black squirrel pauses at the pole's base,
leaps, scrambles up, and stops just below the wires.
Motionless, it looks down on me,
maybe fearing that I will follow.
I move away to calm its fear,
wondering at its purpose in that odd place.
Stepping slowly back, I see the scrawny creature,
hanging upside down, peeling and gobbling up
what seems to be a walnut,
for small green chunks of husk drop to the ground.

What is its squirrely purpose on this barren pole?
Is it safety or freedom from competition,
as when a dog trots off with its bone?
But hanging by hind legs
and eating upside down thirty feet above the ground
seems a desperate posture for enjoyment
of dinner or solitude—or even for managing surveillance.

I watch until my neck grows sore.
Why does that squirrel seclude itself for dinner?
Does the world of squirrels roil with rivalry and warfare?
Leaving such questions for naturalists, I walk thankfully on.
At least my world retains enough decency and peace that
I have no call to eat my dinner
upside down in fear or isolation.
Well, not yet.

Monochrome Dirge

September, 2020

These days
siding is grey,
rugs are grey,
walls are grey,
clothes are grey—
grey as drooping rainclouds.

Grey is the news,
grey the humor,
grey the politics,
the nation's prospects loom grey—
dull and grey, like a midnight mist.

A smothering pall of grey
stifles our spirits,
chokes our hopes,
and buries our smiles—
a dismal, unnatural pall,
even more dismal, more choking
than any of those ugly,
smile-stifling Covid masks.

Bereaved

Thin, white-fringed daisies,
wind-blown, dry, in weary fields,
mourn their once-bright suns.

Note: *Daisy* was an Anglo-Saxon kenning or metaphor: day's eye (*dæges ēage*) the sun—and also the yellow flower that resembles the sun.

The Gardener

He cuts the flower
with the shrub:
both leaves and blossoms
line his tub.

Such early trimming
fits his scheme:
blooms are but minor,
it would seem:

agenda stands first
in his mind,
and Beauty bravely
halts behind.

His method let us
not ignore:
it holds the force of
metaphor.

In memory of my friend Ronald Kooistra

Today's Tea

Today we will visit Marcia with tea,
our first time since Ron has gone.
The wheelchair will be vacant;
the cookie package will be more full.
I will leave one cup aside,
empty as our hearts for Ron,
who drinks now fully from the perfect cup.

Psalm 116:13

The Seed

Long, long have I lain,
far too long, it seems,
waiting, ever waiting,
in this parching drought.

Buried here in dust,
lacking power to sprout,
dormant and barren,
oh, how long have I lain.

I wait, ever I wait
for sprinkling, however small,
some gentle sprinkling,
that I may germinate
and spring up straight and right—
spring up with flower,
burst forth with fruit,
arise to light—to the Giver of light,
Who holds both the power
of the seed and the wonder of rain.

Treasure

Eye treasure, heart's wealth:
carpets of gold encircle
bare, rain-blacked maples.

Two Tableaus

Tableau I
II Samuel 21

Seven men hang impaled on a rocky hilltop at Gibeah;
Rizpah, mother of two,
guards the bodies from desecration of beasts and birds;
her makeshift tent of sackcloth shields her from the fierce sun
until rain quenches three years of drought;
in the remote distance King David's men set out
to remove and bury the withered, rain-washed corpses,
ending Rizpah's vigil.

Tableau II
I Kings 13

On a desolate road leading to Bethel
a riderless donkey stands bleakly beside
a prophet's body, torn and gory in the dust;
thin and vigilant, a lion guards his bloody prey;
an aged prophet dismounts from his donkey
to rescue the body for burial.

*Person, beast, and circumstance—
all imperfect instruments
for the Great Shaper's perfect work.
Emblems they are of every tool
guided by His steady hand
as He forms His edifice
through time and space
with mystery—
and love.*

Bloodhound

Forlorn of face, of doleful eye,
   the dewlapped bloodhound noses by.
      It holds your scent, and though you try

to slip away, quite like a thief
   it pads behind, grants no relief,
      but tracks you down. Its name is Grief.

Supple and Snug

Star-eyed lovers liken love
to Venus, moon, and dipper;
fitter likeness, though, by far—
an interlocking zipper.

Corpus Christi*

A Consolation

On his torn and tender shoulder
the King of the Jews carried
His blood-blotched scepter of salvation.

The King of Kings bears now
upon that potent shoulder
His glorious mantle of authority.
Yet that same shoulder carries, still,
each lost and dirty straying sheep—
each wandering and willing soul
He came to rescue and to keep.

And, yes, He carries near His spear-pierced side,
His precious, costly lambs—
carries them secure through thorns of time,
bears them in His bosom through the black and fearful void—
carries each one home.

---

* *The body of Christ, as mentioned in John 19:17, Isaiah 9:6, Luke 15:5, and Isaiah 40:11.*

Illustration

Now shame-struck, bare, this maple stands,
compliant to the frost's demands.

    Fierce red and orange it wore in pride,
    (shielding every flaw inside)
    when yesterday the daylight died.

Frost chilled its blood in one quick night,
and sunrise sees it naked, quite—
its glory stripped, its shielding dress
unkempt beneath its nakedness.

"Pride goeth before destruction, and an haughty spirit before a fall." Proverbs 16:18

Detour

A half block away I saw the black hearse,
parked on my side of the street.
When two men emerged from the side door
of the pale house on the corner,
carrying a stretcher across my sidewalk,
I stopped—because I knew:
they were carrying not merely a stretcher,
they were carrying Death.
I did not like Death because I had seen it before—
at Henry's funeral, when our class sat in the first pews,
unable to escape the view of his white, fly-flecked face.

I considered: what if Death is not just ugly but contagious?
If I go near, maybe Death will get *me* this time.
So, I crossed the street to get free
from the passage of Death and its infection
and then crossed back to the schoolyard.

And so my childhood wisdom rescued me—
guided me from crossing paths with Death,
altered my course for months to come,
and saved me from its dire contagion.
I knew that Death could neither walk nor run,
so wisdom taught the lesson, and strictly I obeyed.

Of course, my youthful vision did not see
the subtle transept formed by Death's hushed crossing—
did not conceive the sidewalk pattern of the Cross—
that Cross where Life met Death,
where dying brought us immortality.
More years it takes to see that pattern as the key or gate
that opens to the everlasting Way of Holiness,
the Way that holds no rough nor crooked parts
but (without detour) long extends, all level, smooth, and straight.

Wood Work

Most patiently, through scores of years the Carpenter
has shaped and fashioned this obdurate block of wood,
planed and sanded its raw edges and crude corners.

Day after day with Holy Oil He polishes,
caressingly brings smoothness to the stubborn grain,
while slowly in the heartwood of this headstrong block
obedience and love awaken to His work.

The polishing complete, on that great Day of Days
this wood, by grace, will grace the throne room of His house
with luster rich beneath the fondness of His gaze.

"We are His workmanship." Ephesians 2:10

Dejection

The spirit moans, desiring words;
yet no words come.
The soul laments; yet lips and tongue
stay wholly dumb.

The spirit, clothed in sackcloth black,
chokes, dry with fear.
Its hope grown cold, it craves to weep.
Eyes drop no tear.

What dew, what fresh, reviving rain
will solace bring?
What comfort yet can coax this withered
soul to sing?

Purpose

In late November comes the day
to clean the birdhouse for next year's renters.
Deep within the clutter and complexity
of stalks and string, grass and feathers,
nestle three tan and speckled eggs,
forsaken, cold—beyond all hope of reclamation.
Why did mama sparrow leave them?
Did she fall prey to some marauding hawk or furtive cat,
or did a human presence frighten her away?

Gently I toss away the thick-knit nest with its forsaken eggs.
Long vanished is their promise
for flight and freedom, for song or even struggle—
vanished any hope to taste the precious, trying tangle of existence.

I pause beneath the grey November pall,
obedient to a nudge from deep within
to grieve for any life, however small,
brought to an end before it should begin.

Perversion

In its ripe and ravaging maturity
Evil no longer creeps
but races at more than Mercurial speed,
hurtling round our muddled, well-befuddled globe,
gathering unity and purpose,
garnering wealth and power,
and guiding its grisly course
with that complex, now terrifying,
and ultimately calamitous
God-given gift—
technology.

And the muddled, well-befuddled masses,
when they come to know and fear,
urgently, earnestly whisper, "Why?"

Place of Peace

The mind, much like the flighty honey bee,
will often leap from bloom to bloom
of mental daisy or of buttercup.

> That mind, unsettled,
> darts and pauses,
> lifts and flits,
> unstable—and unable
> to find peace.

Far better that the mind should be
more like the rooted buttercup,
that holds its tranquil yellow face
> up toward the sun,
>> its source of gold,
>>> its place of peace.

"*Thou wilt keep him in perfect peace whose mind is stayed on Thee.*" Isaiah 26:3

Crooked Cross Stitch

A Prosy Ramble

I straighten the Victorian cross-stitch picture a bit—
the one that hangs near the dining room table,
thinking of my mother, whose lovely handiwork it is.

If one of the females in my life were to observe my correction,
it would receive her very particular re-correction—
to which I would willingly agree and submit.
(In the same way I submit willingly, almost reverentially,
to female opinion regarding color—
for every woman is a natural authority on color.
It is curious, though, that their authority
as to precise shades and names of colors
permits them to disagree even with the
equal authority of other females.)
I find these female gifts to be pleasing,
partly because they save me
from making finnicky judgements and ignorant choices.

Now, as concerns the pictures hanging crooked in my mind,
as well as the multitude of snapshots and movies, old and new,
crowding to be displayed in the permanent mental collection,
the Curator requires constant adjustments and deletions.
As I apply myself to the adjustments,
I learn what every janitor or housekeeper knows:
cleanness and good order are temporary,
for dust and clutter and dirt return persistently—almost magically.

Yes, mental housekeeping requires far more effort
than the adjustment of the Victorian cross stitch,
especially because the tools of honesty and humility
prefer to linger in the closet with the dust cloth and the mop.

> *"But be ye transformed by the renewing of your mind."*
> *Romans 12:2*

Survival

"Oh, take heed, my child,"
    the Wise One said.
"When you fall in love,
    don't smash your head."

Golden Dawn

A Carol for the Winter Solstice

This time of year
each day dies young;
night smothers soon
each feeble sun.

Yet night begins
this joyful day
reluctantly
to slip away,

and soon the sun
again will ride
high over head
in strength and pride.

Now, when the Son
His Solstice brings,
the night will flee
His rising wings,

for He will light
His morning skies
with golden dawn
that never dies.

Oxygen

Because the snuffer of circumstance is likely to
smother
your candle

of
happy-
new-year
happiness,
pray for the
pure oxygen
of grace, ever
present and
pervasive in
joy and trial,
ever potent
to help restore
any dead or wavering flame.

www.ingramcontent.com/pod-product-compliance
Lightning Source LLC
Chambersburg PA
CBHW061508040426
42450CB00008B/1525